# JOACHIM ANDER

# Twenty- four Short Studies

## for solo flute

## edited by Edward Blakeman

The Danish flautist Carl Joachim Andersen (1847-1909) enjoyed a career as an orchestral player in Copenhagen, St. Petersburg and Berlin (where he was a founder member of the Berlin Philharmonic Orchestra in 1882) until a disability of the tongue forced him to give up flute playing in 1892. He then made a new career as conductor of the Tivoli Theatre Concerts in Copenhagen and he taught at the Royal Danish Academy of Music. Towards the end of his life he was honoured by the government in recognition of his services to Danish music.

The 24 Short Studies, Op.33, were composed during Andersen's time in Berlin and published there and in New York in 1888. They were dedicated to Jac de Jong, solo flautist to the Dutch Court in Amsterdam, and the title page announces that they had been adopted as teaching material by the Music Academies of Berlin, Dresden, Hamburg and Leipzig. Andersen's obvious concern in these studies for the musical, as well as the technical development of the flautist continues to make them rewarding to play. They are of intermediate standard, sutitable from about Grade 6 onwards.

The present edition closely follows the original printing, apart from several minor corrections of accidentals. Most of the studies have very detailed indications of articulation and dynamics. These have been clarified in certain places, but not substantially altered. If carefully adhered to, they provide useful insight into the performance practice of the period.

E.B. 1985

## CHESTER MUSIC

(A division of Music Sales Ltd)
8/9 Frith Street, London W1V 5TZ

# Twenty-four Short Studies

JOACHIM ANDERSEN (Op.33)
Edited by Edward Blakeman

4

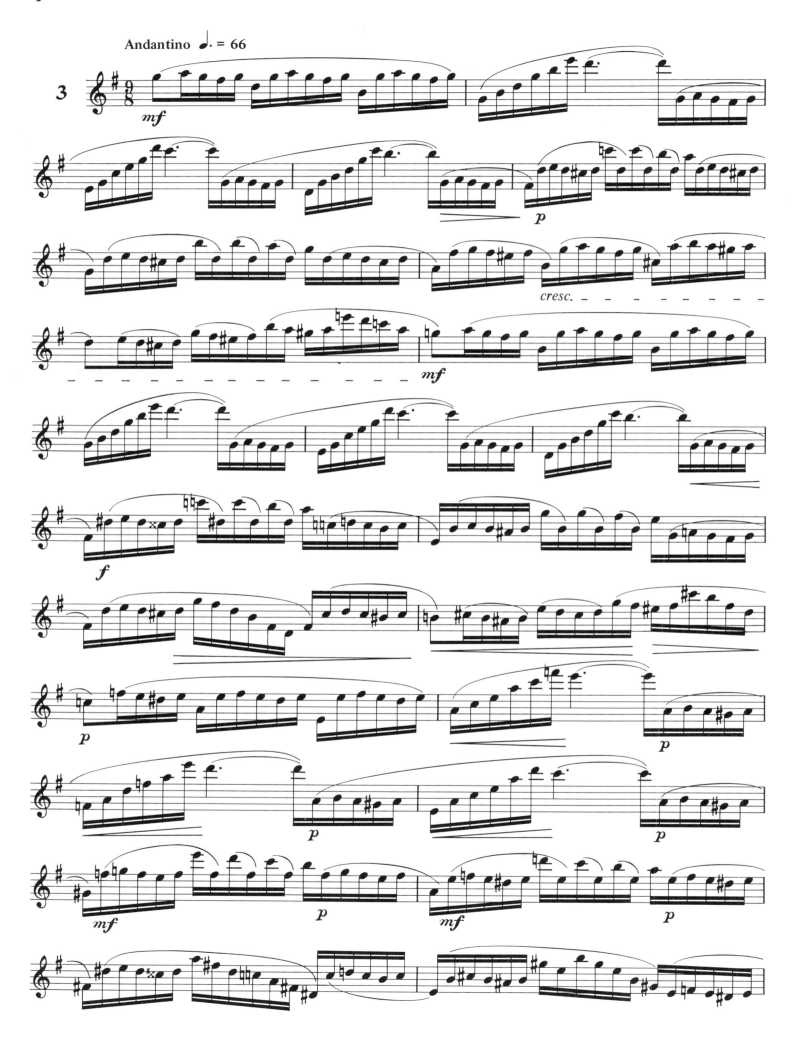

**Allegro moderato** ♩ = 104

**4**

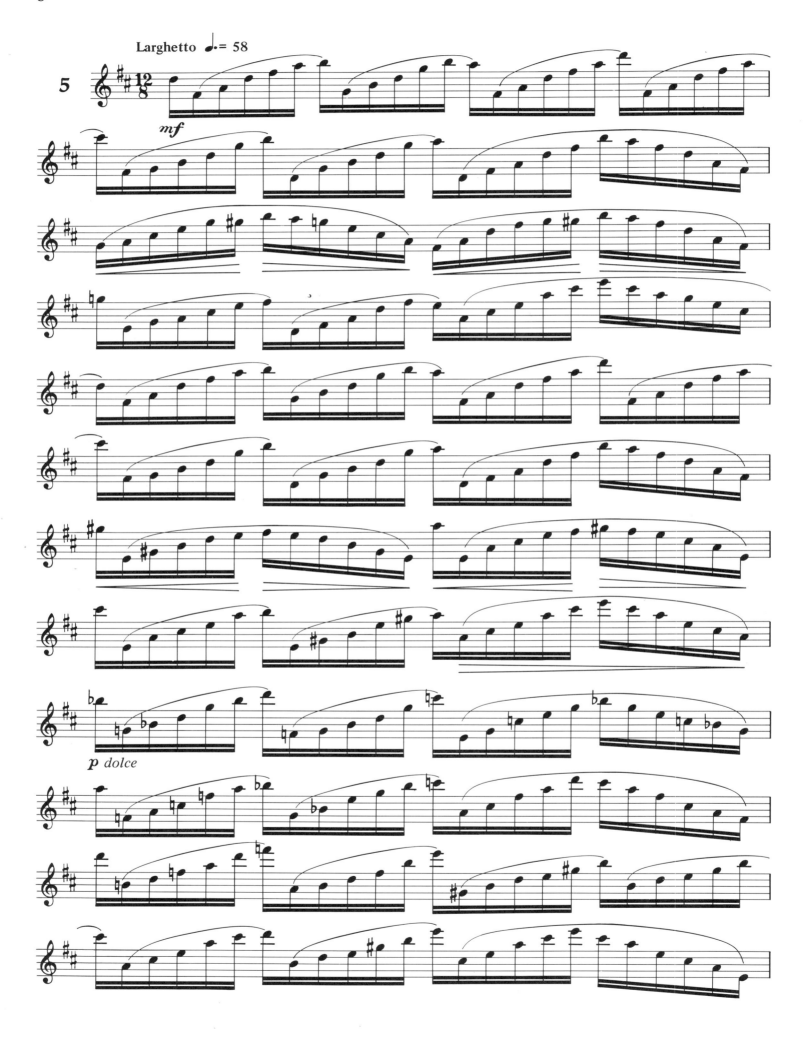

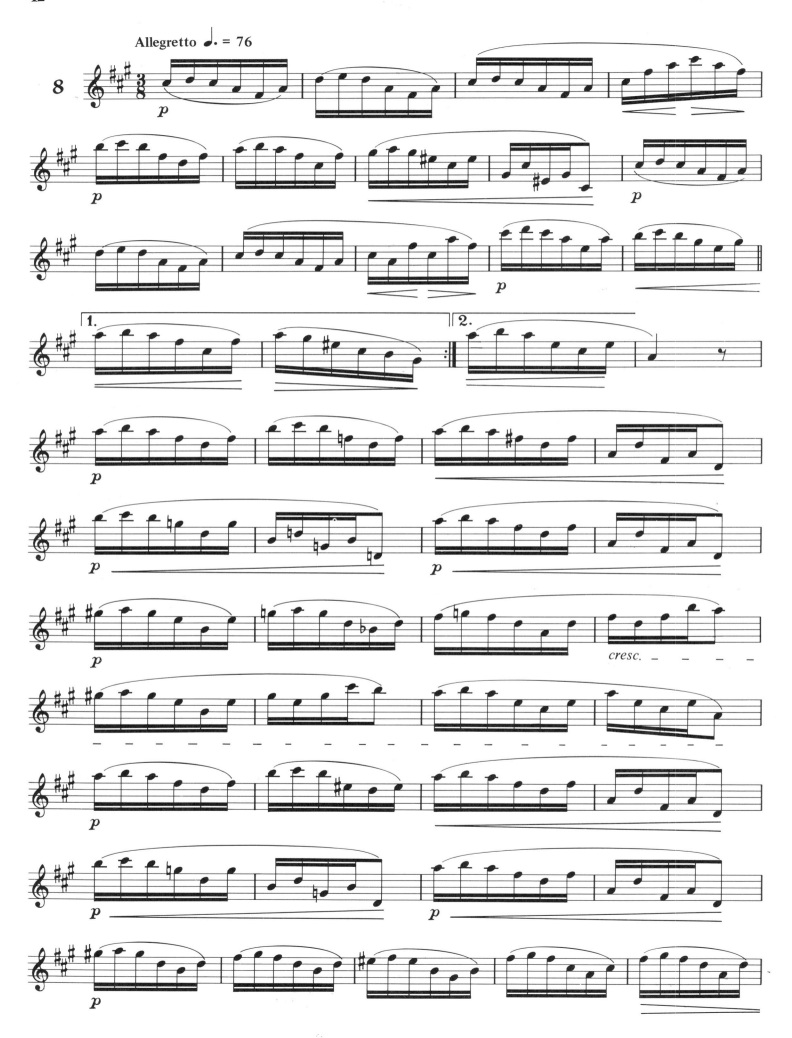

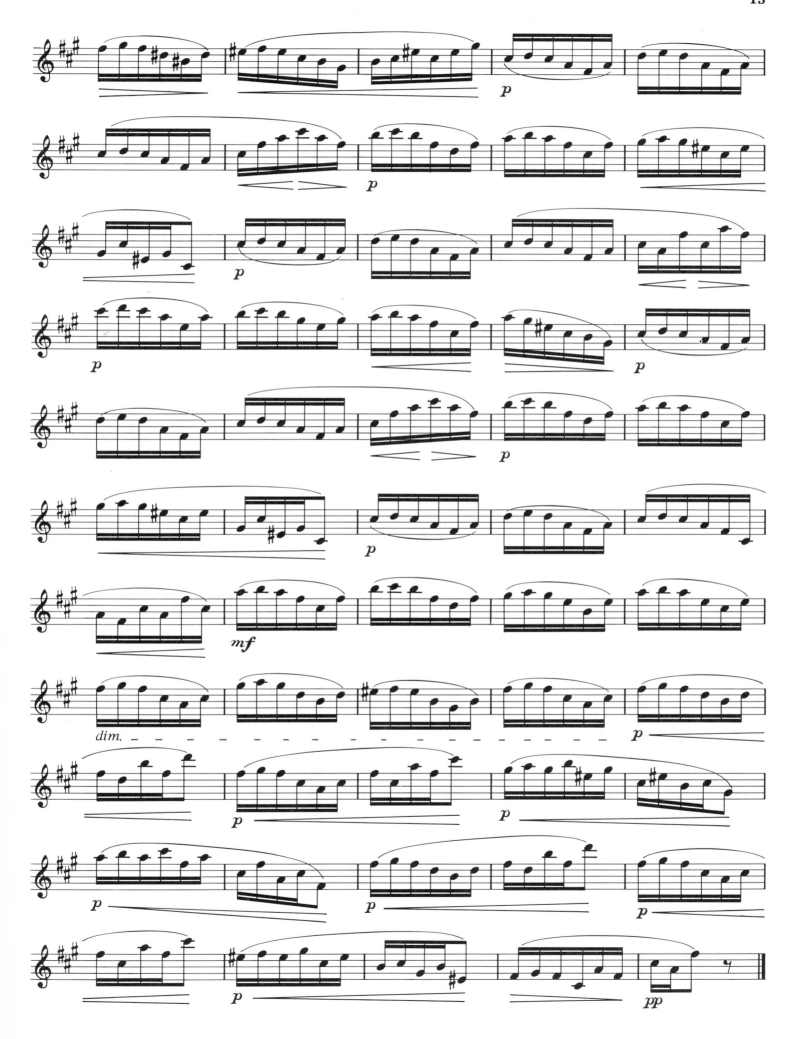

14

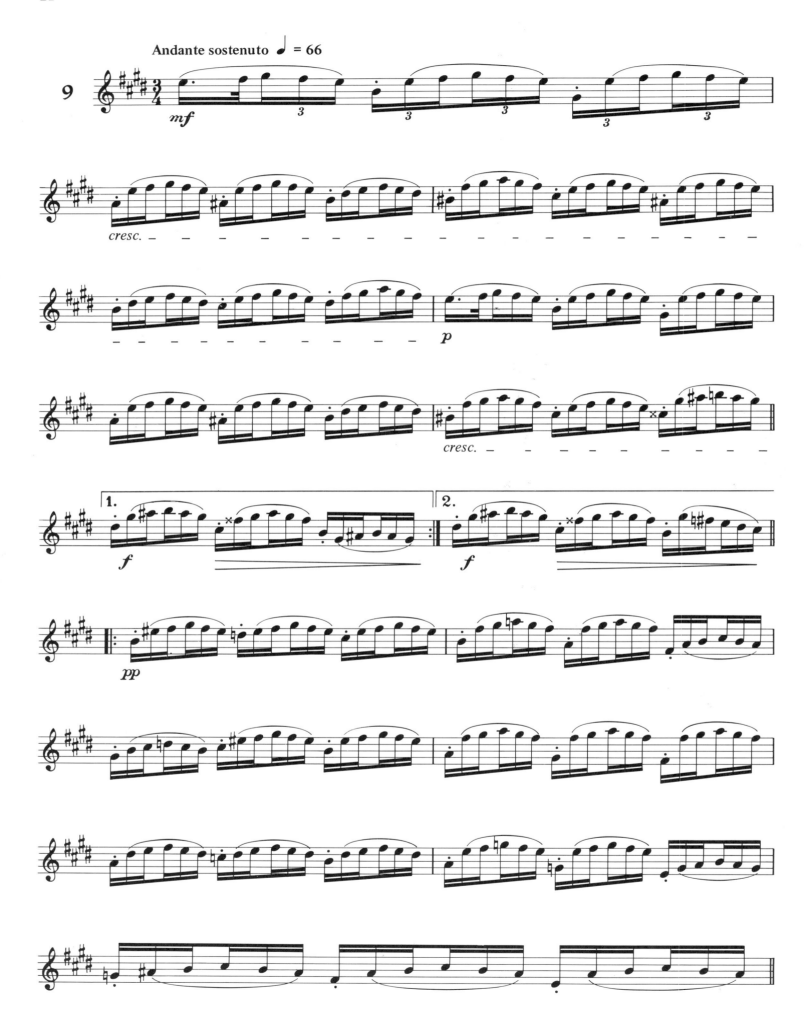

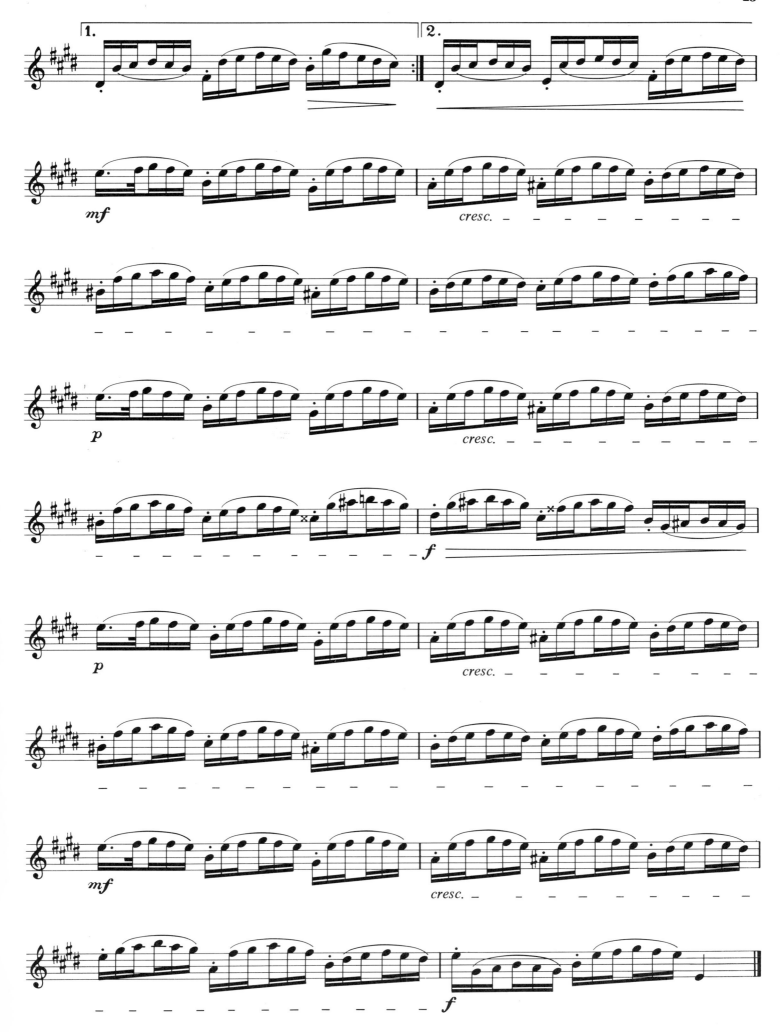

**12**

22

24

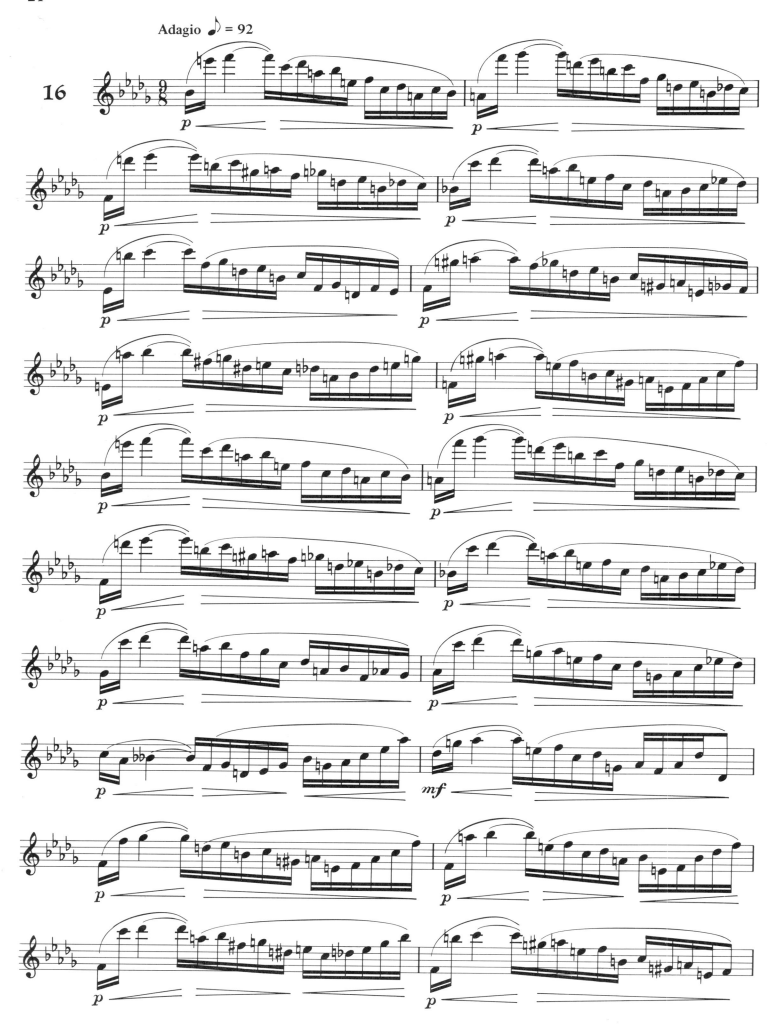

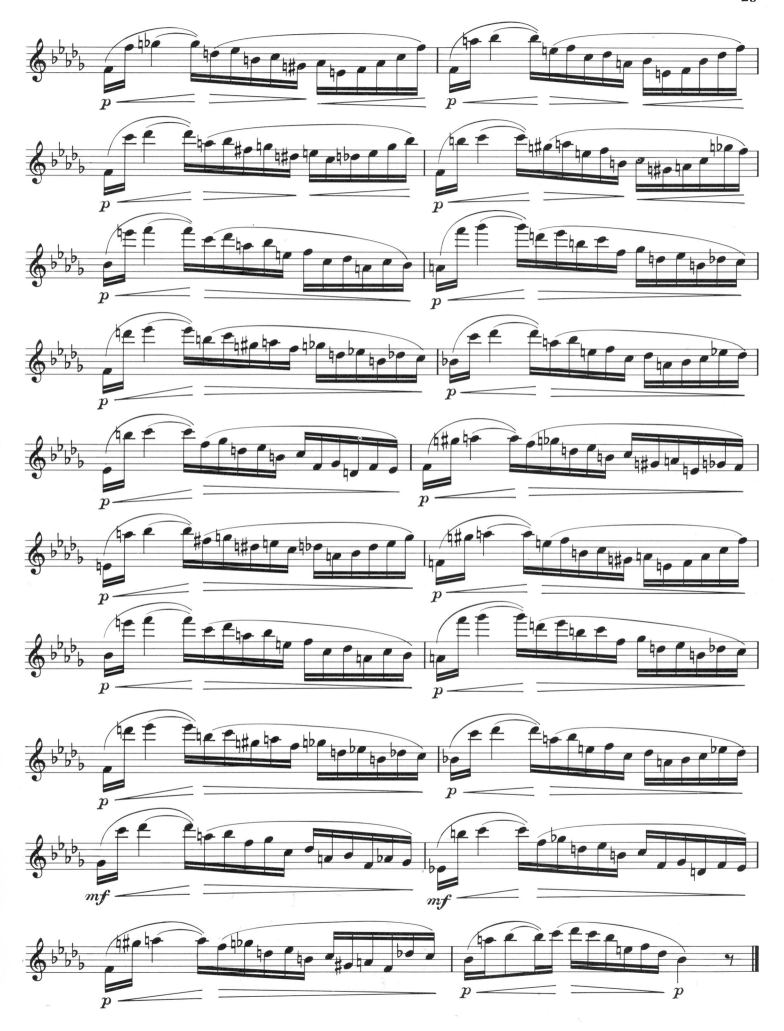

**Allegro moderato** ♩ = 88

**18**

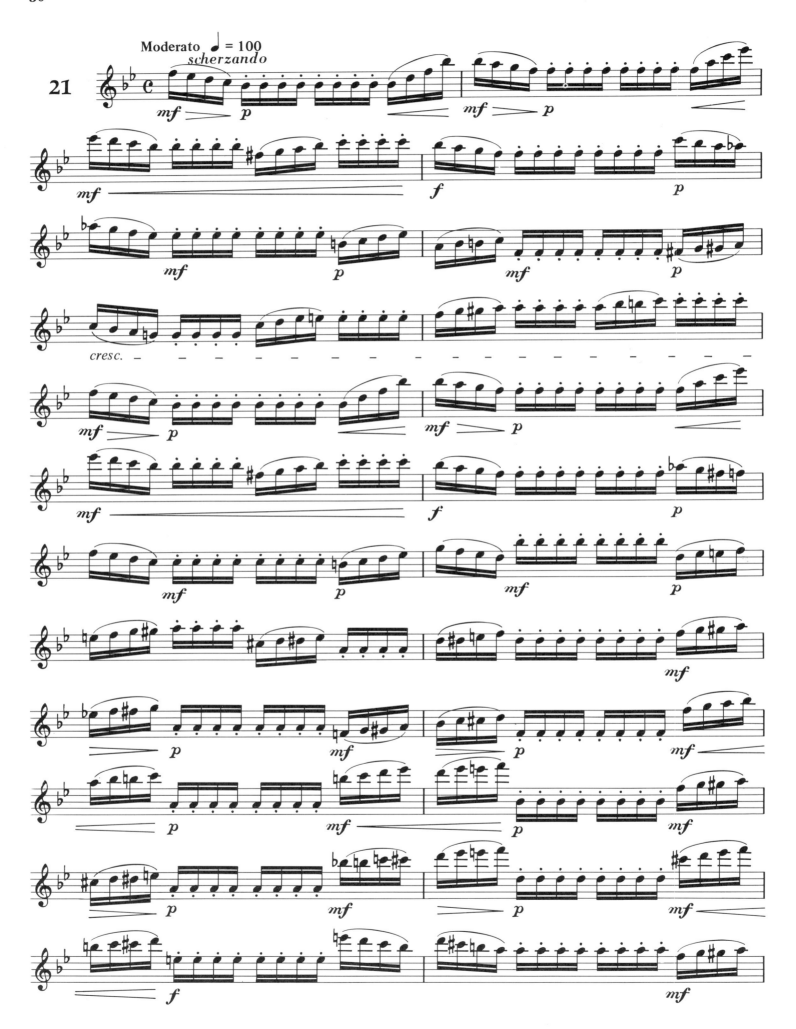

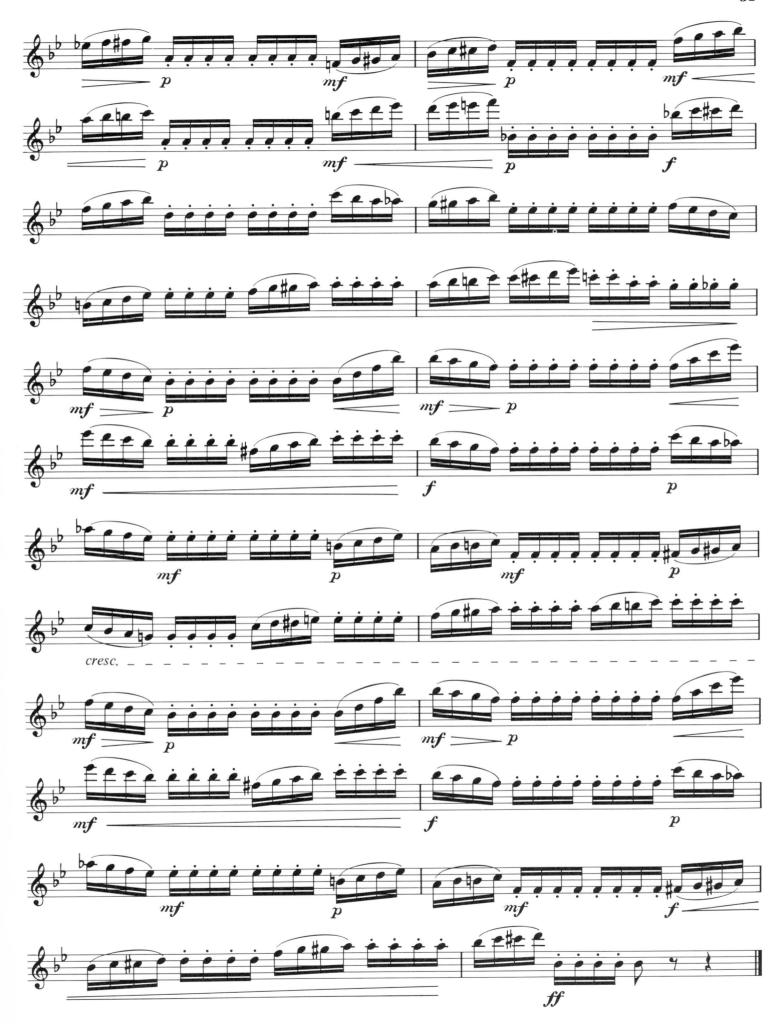

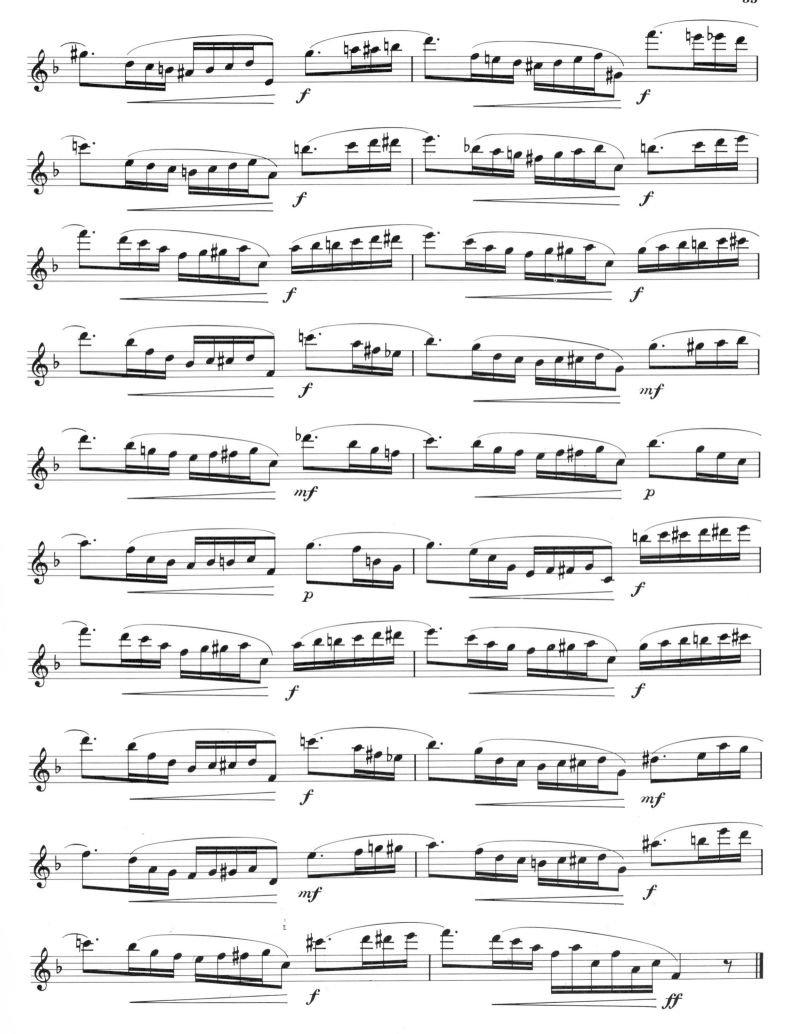

36